BUDDHIST VIEWS

Dieter Glogowski · Albrecht Haag

BUDDHIST VIEWS

CONTENTS

To be born human is very fortunate but rare,
and we should use this precious opportunity as wisely,
skillfully, and effectively as possible.

THE 14TH DALAI LAMA

Thundup Dorje, a farmer, resting by an old prayer wheel in Lingshed Gompa courtyard – winter 1998

Message of His Holiness the 14th Dalai Lama

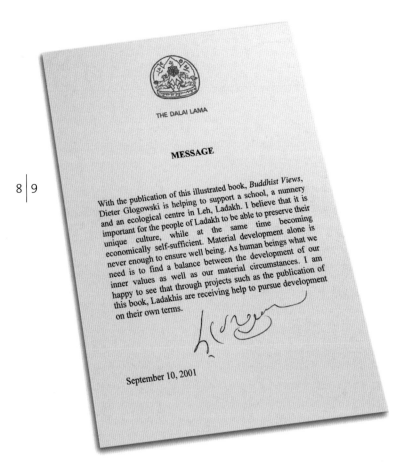

With the publication of this illustrated book, *Buddhist Views*, Dieter Glogowski is helping to support a school, a nunnery and an ecological center in Leh, Ladakh. I believe that it is important for the people of Ladakh to be able to preserve their unique culture, while at the same time becoming economically self-sufficient. Material development alone is never enough to ensure well being. As human beings what we need is to find a balance between the development of our inner values as well as our material circumstances. I am happy to see that through projects such as the publication of this book, Ladakhis are receiving help to pursue development on their own terms.

SEPTEMBER 10, 2001

"Remember to Remember"

The transmission shifted into gear with a bang, the engine groaned and the exhaust was churning out dark black smoke. Norbu was laughing. With all his might he was turning the steering wheel, the road winding endlessly. "Tserka ma cho, na gadi sulte lo sum song – Don't worry, I've been driving this stretch for three years now!" The river Indus was meandering deep down below, our wheels were a hand's breadth away from the precipice. The tattered old bus was filled to the brim with all kinds of people from all parts of the Indus valley: Ladakhi women, Zanskari farmers, Indian soldiers, Kashmiri traders, nuns, monks and children. In the aisle bags full of staple food were piled up. A goat was chewing and resting its head on my leg. Hopefully its stomach would not get upset in the bends.

"Life is precious, drive slow!" I happened to read this slogan while we were shooting past a rock-face. A little farther ahead:

"Better late than dead!" There was just enough room for a single vehicle on the road. "Yes, Indian people know how to build Himalaya roads!" An obese Indian man in the neighboring seat was trying to calm me down. Simultaneously, a wrecked car in the valley down below us just caught my eye! "My name is Bova Shavi, I am from Kulu". Introducing himself, he had squeezed in between Albrecht and me. It was somewhat disturbing to acknowledge that the bench was meant for three persons! To avoid the musical entertainment coming from speakers that were fully overstrained, we used chewing gum as ear plugs. Norbu was signalling: five more hours to Leh! Riding a local bus in India is an adventure of the special kind. Glancing through the window, I was speechless: The barren high plateau of Ladakh displaying its own particular charm. Sun and clouds playing their ever changing game of light and shadow. Chortens,

Landscape of chortens before the mountains of Zanskar – summer 1994

shining white relic shrines gleaming in the scenery, prayer flags moving with the wind. I got caught up in dreams.

15 years ago, I had travelled to Ladakh for the first time. I had toured the land of high passes on ancient caravan trails and came into touch with Lingshed Monastery. A six-days walk, far from any motorway, it lies secluded in between Ladakh and Zanskar at 13,000 ft. Rather unreal in appearance, it is truly a mystical place of solitude and silence. Lingshed got me under its spell.

In the summer of 1993, a very special kind of encounter occurred. The air was clear and there was not one single cloud in the sky when I crossed Hanumala pass at dusk. Lingshed nestled in the valley down below, awaiting me. I negotiated the familiar descent from the chorten on the high pass down to the village. The moon was shining over the old monastery, candle light flickering from the windows of the monks' quarters. Beside the chorten portal I settled down for the night. Next morning, suddenly there he was: "Julley, my name is Geshe Lama Ngawang Changchup, how are you?" I peeped out of my sleeping bag: there was a tall monk above me with

an incredibly warm-hearted smile, a feeling of closeness came up from deep inside me. "You like to have tea in my room?" This was the beginning of a deep friendship that was going to change my life.

My body was shaken, the brakes screeching, the bus engulfed by a cloud of dust, oncoming traffic and a military convoy! Impossible! They would never be able to pass each other on this narrow road! Deep below the tributary waters of the river Zanskar flowed to the Indus. Norbu was maneuvering the bus as far out as possible and turned the music off – it seemed to be getting serious. A humming sound came up in the bus: "Om mani padme hum, om mani padme hum …" the mantra of Avalokiteshvara, the buddha of compassion. Cold sweat was showing, on the forehead of the Indian man who sat next to me as well. I assumed that in this instant he would give anything if "India's best road builders" had constructed the road just one meter wider in this spot! For the first time Norbu was under pressure. Part of the rear twin tire was in the air already, any further and the game was up. Slowly the army vehicles were squeezing past one by one, some nearly touching the side of our bus, which was quite dented anyway. Time

Geshe Lama Ngawang Changchup and a novice monk called Stenzing with Lingshed Monastery in the background – fall 2001

seemed to stop. The murmuring of the mantra became more intense. I was counting 17 vehicles! At last they had all passed! "Life is suffering," Norbu shouted in my direction, switched the music on again and shifted into first gear. Very true: life is suffering. Three hours to go to Leh. The Dalai Lama was smiling gently at me. Norbu had put his photograph over the driver's seat.

We were passing through a small village. A hotel sign read: "e-mail, continental food, hot water running 24 hours." The bus stopped – 15 minutes tea break. I found a matching quote of the Dalai Lama in my note book: "Traditional rural societies may seem very attractive, but on the other hand their people should not be excluded from the advantages of modern development. At the same time such development and progress should not be one-sided. Members of traditional communities like the Ladakhi people generally experience an inner development which makes them warm-hearted and contented. We would be wise to copy them in that way." Norbu came up to me and asked: "Acho, chai?" – "Yes, I would like a cup of tea," I replied.

We had had a long conversation then, Geshe Lama Ngawang Changchup and I. We were talking about Tibetan Buddhism, about spiritual life in Lingshed valley, but also about the changes going on in Ladakh. Geshe-la was born in Lingshed into a poor farming family. At the age of 13 he entered the monastery, enthusiastic to study. Already five years later he went to the Tibetan monastery in exile Drepung in South India. There he studied Buddhist philosophy for 25 years and took the Geshe exam in the presence of the 14th Dalai Lama and in front of 10,000 monks. Since 1992, Geshe-la has returned to Lingshed for three months every summer. In 1993, he founded the "Welfare and Social Society of Lingshed." Since then he has supported the construction of schools, helped the local "Amchi" doctors to develop the traditional Tibetan medicine and made a dream come true: the construction of a nunnery in Lingshed.

The shrill sound of the horn announced: tea break finished! What a diversity of religions in our bus – Moslems from Kashmir, Buddhists from Ladakh, Hindus from India. In Leh there is even a Christian Herrenhuter congregation. Didn't Gandhi once write from his prison cell: "Having studied the main religions as hard as I was able to, it occurred to me that there must be a key to the common basis of all religions, in case it is meaningful and necessary at all to discover their common interest. This key is truth and nonviolence."

Chugging along, our bus was taking the final ascent. In front of us the plain valley of Leh was visible. From the side of the valley on the left, Phiyang Monastery was shining brightly. Slowly the sun was sinking behind the icy peaks of the Transhimalaya. My Indian co-traveller next to me was snoring away into my ear with seeming pleasure and the goat had buried its head up to the neck in my jacket. We had almost reached Leh. On a hill to the right I recognized Spituk Monastery surrounded by Indian army barracks – compassion and violence contrasting most obviously. The Dalai Lama kept smiling from above the driver's seat, a loving warm smile showing his irresistible sense of humor. How convincing had been his speech way back in fall 1998 in the city of Bonn in Germany: "It is getting more urgent that we acknowledge mental and spiritual life as the actual reliable basis to attain true happiness and peace."

The year 1998, marked by Ladakh and Tibetan Buddhism, had made a deep impact on my life. We were filming two documentaries about Zanskar and Ladakh for the German TV station of Hesse. Geshe-la's second visit to Germany was coming up as well as my photo exhibition on Lingshed people's lives. What was special about that was that the photographs were connected to contemplative spiritual quotations – the idea for the book "Buddhist Views" was taking shape. So, how to distinguish between the Buddhist view and other views? Sogyal Rinpoche, a master of the Nyingma tradition, likes to put it this way: "When Jesus met Buddha he asked: 'What is it actually that is separating us?' – 'Our fans,' replied the Buddha."

The Dalai Lama calls it 'compassion,' Gandhi says 'truth' and 'nonviolence,' Jesus 'charity.' For many years I had collected quotations of great bodhisattvas for this book. Among them I include the 14th Dalai Lama as well as Thomas Merton, Thich Nhat Hanh, Hildegard von Bingen, Meister Eckhart, Rainer Maria Rilke, Mother Teresa, Albert Einstein, and Bhagwan Shree Rajneesh. Quotations on compassion, love, meditation, on dying, delusion, hatred, and craving. Quotations bringing clarity – guides to inner peace. Quotations helping not to forget the main thing: "Remember to remember that you remember" (Sogyal Rinpoche, Kirchheim, 1996).

DIETER GLOGOWSKI, LEH, APRIL 2002

pp 16/17: **The capital Leh and its royal palace** is embedded in the Indus valley at 11,000 ft – spring 2002
pp 18/19: **Chortens and prayer flags** are important features in the Himalayan scenery – spring 2002
pp 20/21: **Landscape of chortens** near Shey Monastery – spring 2002

BUDDHISMUS IN LADAKH

Even when setting out for the five-day trek to Leh, like Tsewang, none of the monks from Lingshed Monastery, take any of the short cuts. According to ancient Buddhist tradition he passes each and every chorten in his way on the left hand side. And – Ladakh is dotted with chortens, the holy relic shrines of the Buddhists.

Everyday spirituality

In this matter, wearing the dark red monk's robes does not make a difference. Every believing Ladakhi – almost 90 percent of the total population – behaves exactly like Tsewang, not just when it comes to passing chortens. Spirituality, religious ritual and everyday life in Ladakh are inseparably intertwined, and it is precisely this relation which reflects the people's life and heart. Everywhere, be it in the villages or in the uninhabited valleys, one encounters the monuments and signs of a deep rooted philosophical view of life. There is not a day without the echoes of the "Om mani padme hum" mantra

resounding in the mountains, or the thousands of prayer wheels rattling, and the genuine closeness of people with smiling faces.

A little bit of history

It is not that the Buddhist way of thinking spread overnight or was implemented as a solid doctrine. On the contrary – it underwent various disseminations and numerous modifications until, recently, it has even reached the western world.

First dissemination

Thanks to the Indian Emperor Ashoka, the philosophical movement was brought to Ladakh two hundred years after the passing of the historical Buddha Shakyamuni, as early as three hundred years before the Christian era. As he was extremely enthusiastic about the Buddhist teaching, Ashoka sent scholars to all the corners of the empire to have Buddha's world view spread. Starting from Buddhist seminaries in

A monk on his way to Lingshed Monastery – fall 2001

Kashmir the teachings slowly reached the Himalayan region of Ladakh, the land of the high passes, which today is part of India's most northern district Jammu & Kashmir.

Encounter with the Bon tradition

Here the teachings of the Buddha met with the Bon religion, a popular belief strongly characterized by animistic and magical features. People thought that nature was populated by gods and demons, which could be controlled exclusively by the bonpos, a kind of shamans. At least according to legend it is said, thanks to the great tantric scholar Padmasambhava from Udyana in north-western India, that the clash with the belief in demons lead to integrating Bon elements into the Buddhist ways in the eighth century CE. It was also said that he alone, appearing in one of his eight different emanations, some of which are highly wrathful, had been able to hold back the animistic forces by his magical power. This is why, in Ladakh, even today giant footprints longer than three feet are venerated as his.

Second dissemination

Padmasambhava did not only pave the way for Buddhism to make its breakthrough in Ladakh, but from Ladakh it continued to spread into Tibet, which had been left untouched by Buddhism even though more than a thousand years had passed since Buddha Shakyamuni's activities. With the growing influence of Islam the seminaries in Kashmir lost their importance. Tibet became the center of Buddhist philosophy and Ladakhis were directing their interest increasingly toward the east. Not only the trade routes through the Himalayan region accounted for the exchange of ideas between the two regions, but also many monks from Ladakh went to live in the monasteries of Tibet, to the effect that spiritual ways in the land of the high passes were highly influenced by Tibet for centuries.

Branches of Buddhist philosophy

As time went by, the teachings divided into three lines of thought: the so-called small vehicle, the Hinayana, the great vehicle Mahayana and within the latter the diamond vehicle, Vajrayana, which took root in particular in the Himalayan region. They differ in certain aspects, but the genuine content of the Buddha's words is common to all of them: "On suffering and its causes I teach, on the path that leads out of this suffering, and on the aim of escaping from the cyclic existence of birth and death, the passing into nirvana."

Tikse, a Gelugpa Monastery in the Indus valley – spring 2002

The Four Noble Truths and the Eightfold Path

Having attained enlightenment, the Buddha taught the Four Noble Truths to show the way out of the sufferings of human existence. The first Noble Truth is that, indeed, life means the suffering of body and mind. The second Truth says that emotions like desire and want, rejection and hatred are governing all human beings preventing them from recognizing the true nature of reality. The third Truth is that there is a way to conquer these mental poisons. The fourth Truth, at last, teaches the Eightfold Path, the way to cut the fetters that bind us to our defective existence. The eight parts of this escape are grouped under three headings: wisdom, moral ethics, and meditation. Wisdom is to know the correct view and develop the proper motivation. Moral ethics is genuine speech, action, conduct, and pursuit. Meditation is mindfulness and concentration.

Hinayana, Mahayana, and Vajrayana

The basic idea of all the three vehicles is to reach liberation from cyclic existence. On this basis, Hinayana works with non-violence, not inflicting any harm on other beings. Mahayana goes beyond this by putting the emphasis on compassion, the wish to help all beings. The ideal of compassion is embodied by bodhisattvas. They follow the Eightfold Path and having reached freedom from the cycle of birth and death, they return in the form of a new emanation to show the path of liberation to others, too. In either case the method is to constantly accumulate karmic merit by positive actions throughout many existences. Vajrayana is an esoteric tantric form of Buddhism with special methods that provide a path to enlightenment within one lifetime. Effective but at the same time high-risk rituals, practices, and tantras not suitable for everybody, form a body of teachings which apply certain codes and which for this reason are kept secret. They are available only to those who have received initiation from a master. Not only in Vajrayana but in Mahayana as a whole, the principles of method and wisdom are of crucial importance: method, which is the practice of compassion in action, and wisdom, which is the direct recognition of the true nature of reality.

All of these three traditions are based on the idea of love and compassion – that is why, in the Buddhist pantheon, Avalokiteshvara, watching us in a kind-hearted way, is one of the most highly venerated deities, for he is regarded as the embodiment of sympathy and goodness.

A smile is the mirror-image of the heart. Norbu Tashi, a Zanskari monk from Stongde in the monastery courtyard – summer 1996

Monastic orders of Tibetan Buddhism

Within Tibetan Buddhism four main monastic orders have developed: Nyingma, Kagyu, Sakya, and Gelug. They vary in terms of ritual practice, the scriptural commentaries they use, and in terms of the meditation deities they prefer. Going back directly to Padmasambhava, the Nyingmapas, also called red-hat school, are the oldest. Their monks have kept the secret magical practices that came down from their tantric master to this day. The only monastery of the Nyingmapas in Ladakh is Trakthok in the village of Sakti where Padmasambhava is said to have stayed for some time.

The order of the Kagyupas is divided into several branches, but they all go back to Marpa, the translator. In Tibet, Marpa's disciple Milarepa is venerated as a national hero. His "Hundred Thousand Songs" count among the most important works of spiritual world literature.

The Sakya order was the first whose lamas had religious as well as secular power. The monks of Matho, the only Sakya monastery in Ladakh, are known to be the most gifted oracles in the country. The yellow-hat school of the Gelugpas is the one that is most widespread in Ladakh. Also in Tibet, before the Chinese invasion in fall 1951, it was the most influential institution, its head, the Dalai Lama, representing secular and religious power at the same time. Lingshed Monastery in Ladakh, the home of Tsewang, belongs to the Gelugpa order as well.

China's population policy in Tibet

The Chinese invasion of Tibet in the fifties had far reaching consequences for both the culture and the religion of the country, because the Chinese had come to stay for good. Radio Bejing called it Tibet's "liberation". As a peace-loving nation Tibet was not very well prepared for the invasion of the "People's Liberation Army."

After negotiations had failed, the 14th Dalai Lama escaped into exile to India in 1959. Within a short time, some 17,000 Tibetans followed him – more than 100,000 to this day. China closed its borders and thus brought any further spiritual exchange between Tibet and Ladakh to an end.

The Five Dhyani Buddhas, a stone relief in the valley of Padum – summer 1998

"Can I contribute anything toward my own enlightenment?"

"Not more than you can contribute to make the sun rise every morning."

"What then is the use of the mind exercises that you prescribe?"

"They take care that you are not asleep when the sun rises."

Anthony de Mello

Scenic sunrise with chortens and the castle of Shey in the Leh valley – spring 2002

When a much larger number of people know the nature of their minds,

they'll know also the glorious nature of the world they are in,

and struggle urgently and bravely to preserve it.

It's interesting that the word for "Buddhist" in Tibetan is "nangpa".

It means "inside-er": someone who seeks the truth not outside,

but within the nature of mind. All the teachings and training in Buddhism

are aimed at that one single point: to look into the nature of the mind,

and so free us from the fear of death and help us realize the truth of life.

SOGYAL RINPOCHE

The monk Tsewang Jorges sitting for his morning meditation – spring 2002 in Shey

As my prayers became more intense and deeper

I had less and less to say.

At last I was completely silent.

I transformed, which is probably an even greater contradiction to talking,

I transformed into someone listening.

At first, I thought to pray was to talk.

But I learnt that to pray is not just to be silent

but to listen.

It is like this: to pray does not mean to listen to oneself talking.

To pray is to become silent

and be silent and wait

until the one who prays can hear God.

SØREN KIERKKEGAARD

Novice monks of Rizong Monastery and their teacher Karma Lobsang – spring 2002 in the Indus valley

Love is like a piece of fruit that is ever ripe to eat.

And it is within the reach of everybody's hand.

MOTHER TERESA

Tashi Mothup and Dolma Tsewa are nuns at Ani Rizong Monastery in the Indus valley near Leh – spring 2002

We should practice meditation softly but steadily,

through-out everyday life, and never miss any opportunity

or any event to look deep into the true nature of life,

which includes our day-to-day problems as well.

If we practice like this, we will stay in close and deep connection with life.

THICH NHAT HANH

Jamyang Lhundup of Matho Monastery is blowing the conch shell to call for puja – spring 2002 in the Leh valley

You can find a strange market place in the stony solitude between the mountains:
There you can exchange life's commotion for sheer limitless bliss.

MILAREPA

Tsewang, the monk, in meditative retreat by the mantra rocks near Shey – spring 2002 in the Leh valley

If I could make prophecies

and knew every secret

and had true realization and full belief

so that I could move mountains,

but missed out on love, I would be nothing.

And if I gave all my belongings to the poor

and had my body burned up,

but missed out on love,

there would be no use for me.

CORINTHIAN 13, 2 UND 3

Novice monks below the giant Maitreya statue of Likir Monastery near Leh in the Indus valley – spring 2002

Where there is trust there is love.

Where there is love there is peace.

Where there is peace there is truth.

Where there is truth there is bliss.

Where there is bliss there is God.

SAI BABA

Novice monk Tashi Namgyal of Phiyang Monastery in the valley of Leh – spring 2002

ༀ་ལ་གི་ཕུ་ར་མུ་ས

From the Indus Valley to Lingshed

Scraping the rock-face the trekking bags gave an alarming sound. Slowly the horses were groping their way. The path had been cut into the rocks with great effort, broken patches mended with logs and stones. The horse men's shouts were echoing through Hanupatta gorge. The sun was burning down without mercy. "Nyima nyi Senge-la," horseman Tashi was shouting in my direction. Silently I nodded back, gasped for breath and concentrated on the trail. Within two more days, we would take the 16,000-ft Senge pass. Lingshed was still a four-days walk ahead, six more passes to cross, which is not surprising if you know what the word "Ladakh" means: "la" means pass and "dakhe" means land. The land of high passes!

When we reached the spot to spend the night at the end of Hanupatta gorge we were exhausted. Packhorses had to be unsaddled, water to be fetched and a fire place set up. The night was clear, shooting stars made us utter secret wishes. I crawled deep down into my sleeping bag. "Happiness is not a place, it is a path to follow," said Thundup Dorje , the old farmer, gently smiling in my heart. I was wondering how he was keeping. Winters are bitterly cold in Zanskar – it is a life of want. Still he had never lost his sense of humour, deep lines of laughter were engrained into his face. His good heart and his contentment had made a strong impression on me, as much as the beautiful sunflowers in his garden.

Several days later we were crossing the last of the high passes. Lingshed was spreading out below. What a spectacular scenery: green barley fields, houses dotted about here and there, protectively surrounded by the barred mountains of the Transhimalayan range. Novice monks came running to greet us, monks were lining up in front of the monastery holding kataks, the white ceremonial scarfs of the Tibetans. In the crowd I recognized Sonam Dorje, his eyes gleaming with joy.

Hanupatta gorge between Wangla and Photoksar – fall 2001

No matter how many holy words you read;

No matter, how many you speak –

What is their use for you, if you do not act accordingly?

DHAMMAPADA

"Om mani padme hum" – mani stones up on Senge-la (Lion's pass) – spring 2002

Learn to seize the present moment! Do not steal away.

Do not escape into the delusions of the past or the future.

Focus your mind on where you are, with a keen consciousness
directed at the present moment.

This is where we are.

There is no other place than here.

Drukpa Rinpoche

Overlooking Zanskar from the Lion's pass (Senge-la) – fall 2001

Right here and right now we experience real life.

The past has already gone, the future has not yet arrived.

In the present moment only can we really touch life.

THICH NHAT HANH

A human being is part of a whole, called by us the "Universe," a part limited in time and space.

He experiences himself, his thoughts and feelings, as something separated from the rest —

a kind of optical delusion of his consciousness.

This delusion is a kind of prison for us, restricting us to our personal desires

and to affection for a few persons nearest us.

Our task must be to free ourselves from this prison by widening our circles of compassion

to embrace all living creatures and the whole of nature in its beauty.

Albert Einstein

What is the difference between a scientist,

who examines life's smallest features under a microscope,

and the old farmer, hardly able to read and write,

who in spring time roams his garden thoughtfully and watches

a flower opening on the twig of a tree?

For both of them life is a complete mystery.

One can describe it more detailed than the other,

but it is equally unfathomable for both of them.

Any knowledge is knowledge about life, after all,

and all realization is to marvel at life's mystery.

ALBERT SCHWEITZER

Farmer Thundop Dorje in his garden – summer 1998

In Buddhism mindfulness is the key to everything.

Mindfulness is the energy that casts its light on every thing and on every activity;

it gives rise to the power of concentration, it leads to deep insight and to

awakening. Mindfulness is the basis of any Buddhist practice.

THICH NHAT HANH

Tsering Yangchen bidding welcome to her farmhouse in Lingshed in the traditional way – summer 1998

The birth of a man is the birth of his sorrow.

The longer he lives, the more stupid he becomes,

because his anxiety to avoid unavoidable death becomes more and more acute.

What bitterness!

He lives for what is always out of reach!

His thirst for survival in the future makes him incapable of living in the present.

CHUANG-TZU

Dolma, 10 years old, with her little sister Tashi Tsering in Lingshed – summer 1996

This existence of ours is as transient as autumn clouds.

To watch the birth and death of beings

is like looking at the movements of a dance.

A lifetime is like a flash of lightning in the sky,

rushing by, like a torrent down a steep mountain.

SHAKYAMUNI BUDDHA

Farmer woman Tashi Choszan on the way to her barley field in Lingshed – fall 2001

When you are strong and healthy,

you never think of sickness coming,

but it descends with sudden force

like a stroke of lightning.

When involved in worldly things,

you never think of death's approach;

quick it comes like thunder

crashing round your head.

MILAREPA

Thundup Namgyal, a young farmer, and his house "Bando" – summer 2001

As Buddha said,

"What you are is what you have been,

what you will be is what you do now."

Padmasambhava went further:

"If you want to know your past life,

look into your present condition;

if you want to know your future life,

look at your present actions."

SOGYAL RINPOCHE

Grandfather "Meme" Sonam Targes turning his prayer wheel – summer 1994 in Lingshed

Trees and flowers and herbs

grow in silence.

Stars and sun and moon

move in silence.

Silence makes us see things differently.

MOTHER TERESA

Farmer Woman Angmo Tukche spinning wool – summer 1996 in Lingshed

I realized that there are things that every person is sent to earth to realize and to learn. For instance, to share more love, to be more loving toward one another. To discover that the most important things are human relationships and love and not materialistic things. And to realize that every single thing that you do in your life is recorded and that even though you pass it by not thinking, at the time, it always comes up later.

TOLD TO NEAR-DEATH RESEARCHER KENNETH RING

"Meme" Tashi Rigdzin is playing with his granddaughter – summer 1998 in Lingshed

The Dalai Lama talks often of the lack of real self-love and self-respect that he sees in many people in the modern world. Underlying our whole outlook is a neurotic conviction of our own limitations. This denies us all hope of awakening, and tragically contradicts the central truth of Buddha's teaching: that we are all already essentially perfect.

SOGYAL RINPOCHE

Farmer Tsering Andus in the courtyard of Lingshed Monastery – fall 2001

Fear throws our minds into a state of delusion over and over again.

Therefore we are no longer able to get in touch with all the wonderful things of life.

As if there was a wall between us and the world's richness out there,

we have lost our sensitivity for what is holy in the world and cannot reach it anymore.

THICH NHAT HANH

Farmer woman Karma Lekshis with "dor", leaves of barle – summer 1998

Living beings are wandering helplessly in the cycle of existences due to their fundamental ignorance, which is also the ultimate cause of disease. They do not understand the true nature of phenomena, and that is why they are controlled by desire, hatred, and mental obscuration. These mental poisons create habitual tendencies in the mind which, on their part, are the cause of disorders of wind, bile, and phlegm. These disorders of the body fluids' balance finally manifest in the form of countless diseases. This means that for restoring the balance an holistic approach taking into account and comprising features like the seasons, climatic conditions, personality, age, nutrition, behavior, and the environment of the patient is needed.

YESHI DONDEN,
PERSONAL PHYSICIAN OF THE 14TH DALAI LAMA

Sonam Dorje, a doctor of traditional Tibetan medicine, "Amchi", in the process of making drugs – fall 2001 in Lingshed

Why do we live in such terror of death? Perhaps the deepest reason why we are afraid of death is because we do not know who we are. We believe in a personal, unique, and separate identity; but if we dare to examine it, we find that this identity depends entirely on an endless collection of things to prop it up: our name, our "biography," our partners, family, home, job, friends, credit cards … It is on their fragile and transient support that we rely for our security. So when they are all taken away, will we have any idea of who we really are?

SOGYAL RINPOCHE

76 years old Sonam Targes with his prayer wheel and rosary – winter 1998 in Lingshed

One of the chief reasons we have so much anguish and difficulty

facing death is that we ignore the truth of impermanence.

In our minds changes always equal loss and suffering.

And if they come, we try to anesthetize ourselves as far as possible.

We assume, stubbornly and unquestioningly, that permanence

provides security and impermanence does not.

SOGYAL RINPOCHE

"Meme" Tsering Norphel († 2001) watching the course of the sun – summer 1998 in Lingshed

True love embraces a feeling of responsibility,

it accepts the other person just like he or she is,

with all weaknesses and strong points.

It is not love, if we appreciate someone's strong points only.

We must accept the weaknesses as well,

and with our effort, patience, and understanding

we must help him or her to transform.

THICH NHAT HANH

When a man is born, he is tender and weak;

At death he is hard and stiff.

When things and plants are alive,

They are soft and flexible;

When they are dead they are brittle and dry.

Therefore hardness and stiffness are death's companions,

And softness and tenderness are the friends of life.

LAOTSE

Farmer Thundup Namgyal's four months old daughter. The black spot on her forehead is meant to protect her from demons – summer 1996 in Lingshed

"If we have lived before," I'm often asked, "why don't we remember it?" But why should the fact that we cannot remember our past lives mean that we have never lived before? After all, experiences of our childhood, or of yesterday, or even of what we were thinking an hour ago were vivid as they occurred, but the memory of them has almost totally eroded, as though they had never taken place. If we cannot remember what we were doing or thinking last Monday, how on earth do we imagine it would be easy, or normal, to remember what we were doing in a previous lifetime?

SOGYAL RINPOCHE

Nine months old Tsering cozy in the basket on her mother's back, well protected from demons' attacks by the pins on her cap. If in fear, her little soul can escape into one of the Kauri shells – summer 1998 in Lingshed

Who does not seek will not find.

If someone knows the river but does not want to go near,

it won't direct its flow toward him.

But desiring to fetch water, he will have to approach.

HILDEGARD VON BINGEN

Little nun Ani Stanzing praying at the three chortens above Lingshed. They represent the bodhisattvas Avalokiteshvara, Manjushri, and Vajrapani – summer 2001

Contemplating impermanence on its own is not enough:

You have to work with it in your life. Let's try an experiment.

Pick up a coin. Imagine that it represents the object at which you are grasping.

Hold it tightly clutched in your fist and extend your arm, with the palm of your

hand facing the ground. Now if you let go or relax your grip,

you will lose what you are clinging onto. That's why you hold on.

But there's another possibility: You can let go and yet keep hold of it.

With your arm still outstretched, turn your hand over so that it faces the sky.

Release your hand and the coin still rests on your open palm. You let go.

And the coin is still yours, even with all this space around it.

So there is a way in which we can accept impermanence and still relish life,

at one and the same time, without grasping.

SOGYAL RINPOCHE

Geshe-la Ngawang Changchup and old Sonam Targes having laughed away the afternoon – fall 2001 in Lingshed

The Buddha taught that I am my own
master and that all depends on myself.

THE 14TH DALAI LAMA

Tashi Shoron, Stanzing Chosket, and Puntsok Dolma of Lingshed nunnery presenting a photograph
of the 14th Dalai Lama – fall 2001

We should learn to consider the earth as our home.

Once we have realized that we are one,

the earth will become our homeland.

We have to feel responsible for every place on earth.

This is the only way to relieve the suffering we meet these days.

THICH NHAT HANH

Two couples on the way home after the dance – fall 2001

Lingshed – A Monastery With a Long Tradition

Deeply penetrating, the radongs, which are similar to alphorns, were resounding—the monks of Lingshed Monastery were calling for prayers. Surrounded by strange looking rock patterns, the shining white monastic constructions were standing high above the valley basin. The creaking doors of the monks' quarters cut into the silence. Monks and novices were leaving their small lodgings and hurried toward the prayer hall. Low voices murmuring mantras filled the room, the smell of butter tea was in the air, rays of light flooded inside. I was lost in thought.

"Skubum tashi odbar – Happy Place of Fire" the monks called their monastery lovingly. No other than the great translator and monk from West Tibet, Lotsawa Rinchen Zangpo (958–1055) is said to have founded Lingshed Monastery after his return from Kashmir, where he had studied Mahayana philosophy for a long time. Legend has it that he founded a total of 108 monasteries all over Spiti, Ladakh, and Zanskar – 108, a holy number of Tibetan Buddhism. Having proclaimed Puktal as a monastic location in the valley of Padum, he crossed the 4.700 meters high Hanumala pass and spent the night below the ridge. When he was overlooking Lingshed valley he caught sight of a stone burning at a rock wall – the sign to found another monastery at that spot. It did not take long until the first monks came to settle in the valley of Lingshed. The monastic complex as it is today is 500 years old. There are 45 lodgings where senior monks and novices live together. The young monks are not only taught Buddhist philosophy by their masters – there are a lot of worldly jobs to be done as well. Lingshed is a monastery of the reformist Gelugpa order. Until just a few years back, it was a home for 70 monks and 30 novices – to this day the numbers decreased to 36 monks and 15 novices.

Chorten portal below Lingshed Monastery – summer 1998

Lingshed Gompa, situated 3.900 meters high on the border between Ladakh and Zanskar, puts a spell on every visitor. From below the vertical rock wall its white-washed constructions calmly overlook the valley and the settlements in the vicinity – there is an atmosphere of peace and harmony. During the short summer seasons the barley fields sway in the wind, the irrigation canals around the terraced fields are decorated with flowers and yaks graze the lush alpine meadows. In winter time it is not unusual that temperatures fall below 30 degrees Celsius. Then the passes are blocked by snow. Nevertheless, during a six-week long period when winter is at its coldest, some courageous valley residents set out to buy stocks – they travel down below along the 90 kilometers long gorge of the river Zanskar, because this way over the frozen ice cover it only takes a one-week foot march to Leh.

The deep relationship between the village people and the community of monks is reflected on many occasions. Everyday life at Lingshed Monastery not only means to gather four times a day for puja rituals, during which prayers for the benefit of all sentient beings are recited. But also since long the monks have been well respected for their artistic skills, like making paper, painting murals, and creating intricate sand mandalas.

Lingshed Monastery with its monks' quarters down below – fall 2001

Since the development of infrastructure has begun in the seventies, a lot of change has occurred in the Himalayan region. Due to the Kashmir conflict, which has been simmering since 1947, Ladakh and Zanskar, considering themselves as a buffer zone between Pakistan and India, have experienced increasing military presence in the regions toward the borders of China and Pakistan. Not only the machinery of war threatens to destroy the balance of worldly and spiritual life alike: Since 1974, when Ladakh was opened to international tourism, an army of another kind has been invading the land of high passes. There is more than one side to tourism: Financially potent visitors have more than economical influence. There is an obvious and lasting change of social structures. Receptive of modernity, mainly the young are leaving the villages and monasteries. Traditions are fading away, feelings and views of life are overthrown. The identity crisis, which undermines the self esteem of society, can no longer be overlooked – a tragic situation, especially because the cultural influence of this society could inspire of all people those of the western industrial nations to change their thinking. The reconstruction of their value system taking the West as an example ultimately ruins our chances to learn the fundamentals from the Ladakhi people.

Spiritual truth is not something elaborate and esoteric,

it is in fact profound common sense.

When you realize the nature of mind, layers of confusion peel away.

You don't actually "become" a buddha, you simply cease, slowly, to be deluded.

And being a buddha is not being some omnipotent spiritual superman,

but becoming at last a true human being.

SOGYAL RINPOCHE

Gendun Tashi, the abbot of Lingshed Monastery, holding vajra and bell, the symbols of method and wisdom – summer 2001

Blessed who lives without hatred

where hatred and coldness prevail.

Blessed who is free of delusion

when the deluded world is ailing.

Blessed who can breathe freely

letting go insatiable grasping

when the greedy world eats itself up.

Blessed who has chosen poverty

for blissful divine serenity pervades him.

SHAKYAMUNI BUDDHA

Monks during puja in the lhakang, Lingshed Monastery's main prayer hall – summer 2001

This is the way I understand humility.

It is not putting oneself down.

It is the genuine principle of action.

Trying to defend myself

by blaming fate for my distress,

I submit to fate.

Blaming betrayal for it

I submit to betrayal.

But taking the blame on myself

I reclaim my powers as a human.

I have the power to influence that which I am a part of.

I am a part of human society.

There is someone within me, thus, against whom I fight

so that I can let myself transcend myself.

ANTOINE DE SAINT-EXUPÉRY

Monk Dorje Tsering performing the morning puja – summer 1998

As a Buddhist I consider death as an ordinary process. I accept it as a reality
which I am subjected to as long as my earthly existence will last.
As I know that I cannot escape death I see no sense in having fear.
Rather I consider death as a change of clothes and not as the final end.
But death is unpredictable: We do not know when or how it will catch up
with us. Therefore it is wise to get prepared before death will come.

THE 14TH DALAI LAMA

Monk Sonam Gyatso († 2001) reading the scriptures – winter 1998 in Lingshed

Lord, make me an instrument of thy peace;

Where there is hatred, let me sow love;

Where there is injury, pardon;

Where there is doubt, faith;

Where there is despair, hope;

Where there is darkness, light;

And where there is sadness, joy.

O Divine Master, grant that I may not so much seek

to be consoled as to console;

To be understood as to understand;

To be loved as to love;

For it is in giving that we receive,

It is in pardoning that we are pardoned,

And it is in dying that we are born to eternal life.

Amen

A PRAYER OF ST. FRANCIS OF ASSISI

A novice following the puja text – summer 1998 in Lingshed:

Planning for the future is like going fishing in a dry gulch;

nothing ever works out as you wanted, so give up all your schemes and ambitions.

If you have got to think about something – make it the uncertainty

of the hour of your death.

GYALSE RINPOCHE

Monk Sonam Chospel, 95 years old, turning the big prayer wheel in the courtyard of Lingshed Monastery – summer 1998

Every time the losses and delusions of life teach us impermanence they take us a step nearer toward the truth. Even if you fall down from very high, there is only one possible landing spot: the ground of truth. If your practice has given you a certain amount of realization, then falling is no longer a disaster, but it lets you discover your inner refuge.

SOGYAL RINPOCHE

The monks Tsewang Jorges and Tsewang Sandup blowing the radongs – summer 1998 in Lingshed

Learning how to meditate is the greatest gift you can make yourself in this life. For only through meditation you can discover your true nature. And only through meditation you will find the stability and trust you need to live well and die well. Meditation is the path that leads to enlightenment.

SOGYAL RINPOCHE

Monk Tsering Mothup in meditation on the roof of his retreat – summer 1998 in Lingshed

Rely on the message of the teacher,

not on his personality;

Rely on the meaning,

not just on the words;

Rely on the real meaning,

not on the provisional one;

Rely on your wisdom mind,

not on your ordinary, judgmental mind.

SHAKYAMUNI BUDDHA:
THE FOUR RELIANCES

Old monk Tsering Mothup († 1999) and his student Karma Lotus in the courtyard of Lingshed gompa – winter 1995

Whatever joy there is in the world

comes from the wish that others may be happy;

And whatever suffering there is in the world

comes from the wish that we ourselves may be happy.

Shantideva

Counting the mantras recited by means of a mala, a rosary with 108 beads – summer 1998 in Lingshed

Do not force anything,

Let life be profound and non-grasping.

Realize that God opens millions of flowers every day

without putting force on the buds.

BHAGWAN SHREE RAJNEESH (OSHO)

A novice on his way back to Lingshed Monastery – summer 1998

More than any other virtue Buddhism emphasizes unselfishness, which finds its expression in love and caring affection.

THE 14TH DALAI LAMA

Monk Iche Namgyal with three of his students – fall 2001 in Lingshed

Grasping is the source of all our problems.

Since impermanence to us spells anguish,

we grasp on to things desperately, even though all things change.

We are terrified of letting go, terrified, in fact, of living at all,

since learning to live is learning to let go.

And this is the tragedy and the irony of our struggle to hold on:

not only is it impossible, but it brings us the very pain

we are seeking to avoid.

SOGYAL RINPOCHE

Monks Sonam Wangdus and Ngawang Gigmet creating a sand mandala in the Maitreya
hall of Lingshed Monastery – summer 1998

The ability to live in peace with others

and with the world depends to a large extent

on the ability to live in peace with oneself.

Thich Nhat Hanh

Novice Stenzing Lhundup and monk Tsewang in the kitchen of Lingshed Monastery – summer 1998

One powerful way to evoke compassion is to think of others

as exactly the same as you.

"After all," the Dalai Lama explains, "all human beings are the same –

made of human flesh, bones, and blood.

We all want happiness and want to avoid suffering.

Further, we have an equal right to be happy.

In other words, it is important to realize our sameness as human beings."

SOGYAL RINPOCHE

Tsering Wangdus († 1995), a handicapped monk – summer 1994 in Lingshed

If in everyday life we are peaceful, content, and wear a smile,

this will not only be helpful for ourselves but for everybody else.

If we really know what it means to live,

what can be better than starting out on the day with a smile?

If we smile, our consciousness and resolve to live in peace and

happiness are reinforced.

The source of a true smile is an awakened mind.

THICH NHAT HANH

Always having a smile for us – monk Jarnam Zurva and novice Stenzing Lhundup – fall 2001 in Lingshed

Imagine the wide ocean and a golden yoke floating on the surface.

In the depths of the ocean imagine a single blind turtle

which comes to the surface once every hundred years to take a breath of air.

How often would it occur that the turtle would stick its head through the hole

of the yoke when coming up?

The Buddha says that it is even rarer to attain rebirth as a human being.

THE 14TH DALAI LAMA

Deep lines of laughter in the face of monk Thundup Sonam († 1994) – summer 1993 in Lingshed

Never give up, no matter what happens.

Never give up, develop your heart.

Too many circumstances in your country develop the intellect rather than the heart.

Have compassion, not only with your friends, but with all beings.

Have compassion and work for peace.

And I say it once again: never give up.

No matter what happens, do not give up.

THE 14TH DALAI LAMA

In 2001, nine monks left Lingshed Monastery:
four joined the Indian army,
four went to live with their girl friends in Leh,
one opened a business in Padum.

ཨོཾ་རེ་ཙ་རུ་རེ་ཙ་རུ་རེ་སུ་རུ

THE NUNNERY PROJECT

When the "Welfare and Social Society of Lingshed" was founded by Geshe Lama Ngawang Changchup in 1992, also the plan to establish an independent convent was born. Four years of planning and realization were to come: acquisition of land from the villagers, which they did not need for farming; purchase of timber from far away Kashmir; transportation on trucks to Zangla in Zanskar, where it was to be stored until the following winter. Not until the ice-cold month of February was it possible for the monks and farmers to undertake the strenuous task of pulling the logs up to Lingshed over the frozen icy cover of the river Zanskar; transportation across Ladakh's high passes in summer would have been impossible.

The laying of the foundation stone took place in summer 1996, and soon afterwards the first 21 girls were enrolled by their parents. Two of the young nuns, Ngawang Angmo and Ani Choszom, both 16 years old, were sent to Dolmaling Nunnery in Dharamsala by Geshe-la. When they have completed a ten-years course in Tibetan philosophy they are

meant to become the heads of Lingshed Nunnery. In August 1998, ten rooms on the ground floor were ready to be consecrated. Geshe-la bought some more land for growing barley as well as two female yaks. Contrary to the monks' master monastery, whose fields are farmed by the villagers, the nuns are completely responsible for themselves.

Many long hard-working days have passed since then until in the year 2000 the first floor could be completed. Also hundreds of tree seedlings were planted in a mutual effort, dozens of irrigation canals dug and many a slope terraced to gain six new fields. Then the communal kitchen was constructed as well as a prayer hall, which was completed in 2004. All of this has brought Geshe Lama Ngawang Changchup a good step further toward his vision of equal rights in spirituality.

Further information:

www.gruntose.com/asynchronous_school/lingshed/ling.html

Donations account: Friends of Lingshed, Sparkasse Oberhessen, BIC: HELADEF1FRI, IBAN: DE 38518 500 79 114 004 2230

Two Lingshed nuns, Ani Puntsok Dolma and Ani Lobsang Yangzum – summer 1998

THE SOLAR SCHOOL

Several years back, the Austrian architect Christian Hlade accidentally ended up in Lingshed. Fascinated by the beautiful location of the village, he came up with the plan to construct a school that would offer the children better chances for their future. In August 2000, eight years after his first visit, Lingshed village school took up operations. The funds for this model project were raised by the Austrian organisation "Friends of Lingshed." The actual construction of the school was preceded by a long period of cooperation with the villagers during which trust in each other steadily increased. The concept that took shape is simple but ingenious: The five class rooms of the school and additional space for the teachers, all in the traditional Tibetan style, are indirectly heated by solar energy, so that lessons can be held even in winter when temperatures are below minus 30 degrees Celsius. Not only the impressive building has turned out well, but what is similarly important: The villagers identify themselves with the construction.

Further information:

www. solarschule.org; www.lingshed.org; info@solarschule.org

Donations account:

Friends of Lingshed, Steiermärkische Bank und Sparkassen AG, BIC: STSPAT2G, IBAN: AT022081502200407076

Mantren

ཨོཾ་ཏི་བཛྲེ

OM MANI PADME HUM
Mantra of Avalokiteshvara,
the buddha of compassion

ཨོཾ་ཨུ་རྟུ་བཛྲ་གུ་རུ་བཛྲ་སི་བི་ཧཱུྃ

OM AH HUM VAJRA GURU
PADME SIDDHI HUM
Mantra of Padmasambhava
(Guru Rinpoche),
the "Second Buddha"

ཨོཾ་ཝ་གི་ཤྭ་རི་མུྃ

OM WAGI SHWARI MUM
Mantra of Manjushri,
the buddha of wisdom

ཨོཾ་བཛྲ་པཱ་ཎི

OM VAJRA PANI HUM
Mantra of Vajrapani,
the buddha of activity

ཨོཾ་ཏཱ་རེ་ཏུ་ཏཱ་རེ་ཏུ་རེ་སྭཱ་ཧཱ

OM TARE TUTARE TURE SOHA
Mantra of Tara, the female
emanation of compassion

Glossary

142 | 143

Amitabha One of the five Mahayana meditation deities derived from the original buddha. He is the source of light and of life.

Ashoka Emperor of the Maurya dynasty in the third pre-Christian century. He converted to Buddhism and united India.

Avalokiteshvara Meditation deity and bodhisattva. Personification of the energy of active compassion. Tibet's patron saint.

Bodhicitta The twofold motivation for liberation: to attain enlightenment through wisdom – for the benefit of all living beings through compassion.

Bodhisattva Mahayana or Vajrayana practitioner with bodhicitta motivation on the path of enlightenment. Also an emanation of a fully enlightened being helping others on the path.

Bon Pre-Buddhist popular belief in Tibet. Natural religion with animistic and magical elements.

Buddha Literally the awakened one. Enlightened being having transcended the sufferings of cyclic existences. Siddhartha Gautama under the name of Buddha Shakyamuni is considered the historical Buddha of our era and the initiator of the Buddhist religion; he was born 560 before Christ in Lumbini/Nepal and attained enlightenment under the bodhi tree in Bodhgaya/India. The Buddha, the Dharma (the Buddha's teachings), and the Sangha (the community of his disciples) are the three objects of refuge (Three Jewels) for practicing Buddhists.

Chorten Tibetan for stupa. Buddhist relic shrine.

Dalai Lama "Ocean of Wisdom". Honorific title given 1578 by the Mongols to the secular and spiritual leader of Tibet, whose reincarnation lineage has been unbroken to this day.

Dhammapada Old Buddhist text containing the main essence of the Buddha's teachings.

Dorje See Vajra.

Drukpa Rinpoche Great Tibetan master of recent history and close confidant of the Dalai Lama. In 1959, he escaped from Tibet; after a period of teaching in Dharamsala, he began teaching at the Nagarkot Monastery in Nepal 1970 until he passed away in 1989.

Eightfold Path The path taught by the Buddha to transcend the suffering of cyclic existences in eight interconnected steps: right view, right intention, right speech, right action, right livelihood, right pursuit, right mindfulness, right concentration.

Gelug One of the four main lines of Tibetan Buddhism, initiated by the monastic reformist Tsongkhapa, also called yellow-hat school.

Geshe Honorific title, mostly for a Gelugpa monk who having completed his studies and exams is authorized to teach.

Geshe-la Geshe Lama Ngawang Changchup. Spiritual head of Lingshed Monastery in Ladakh.

Gompa Tibetan for monastery.

Hinayana Small vehicle. In the Buddhist tradition a path which leads to the individual's liberation from the sufferings of cyclic existence mainly through the practice of non-violence or non-harming.

Kagyu One of the four main lines of Tibetan Buddhism, initiated by Marpa, Milarepa's master.

Lama Tibetan for spiritual teacher.

Mahayana Great vehicle. The Buddhist path aiming at liberation and enlightenment for the benefit of all beings. See bodhicitta and bodhisattva.

Maitreya Buddha of a future era.

Manjushri Meditation deity and bodhisattva of highest wisdom, depicted with the sword of wisdom and the scriptures.

Mantra Phrase used for meditation. Mostly it is repeated over and over again to protect the mind from negative thinking.

Marpa 1012–1098. Tibetan lama and initiator of the Kagyu lineage. Disciple of Naropa and master of Milarepa.

Milarepa 1040–1123. Tibetan yogi. Disciple of Marpa, who put extraordinary hardships on him before he gave him the teachings.

Middle Way The teachings of the Buddha is to be understood as the Middle Way because it does not accept any extremes, be it asceticism which is too strict, or indulgence which is excessive. The philosophical system of the Middle Way avoids the extremes of eternalism and of nihilism through the unity of wisdom and compassion.

Naropa 956–1040. Indian tantric. Disciple of Tilopa, who taught him yogic practices which have been transmitted as the Six Yogas of Naropa.

Nirvana Liberation from the sufferings of cyclic existences.

Nyingma One of the four main lines of Tibetan Buddhism, going back to Padmasambhava and the first translations of the Buddha's teachings from Sanskrit. Also called red-hat school.

Om mani padme hum Literally and roughly translated: Oh, jewel of the lotus. The Mantra of Avalokiteshvara is considered the most often recited in the world. It is about the unity of wisdom, symbolized by the lotus, and compassion, symbolized by the jewel.

Padmasambhava "The Lotus-born" tantric from India, also called Guru Rinpoche. Through his power to pacify demons and spirits he paved the way for the Buddhist philosophy to take root in the Himalaya region.

Puja "Veneration," "ceremony," "ritual," or "service."

Rinpoche Tibetan for precious one, form of addressing a reincarnate lama.

Sakya One of the four main lines of Tibetan Buddhism, called like the seat of their master monastery in Tibet.

Shantideva Indian bodhisattva in the 8th century CE and representative of the Middle-Way philosophy. His main treatise is called "Bodhicaryavatara – Entering the Way of the Bodhisattva."

Sogyal Rinpoche Lama of the Nyingma order who teaches in the West. Jamyang Khyentse Chokyi Lodro, a master of all schools of Tibetan Buddhism, recognized him as a reincarnation of Lerab Lingpa Terton Sogyal, a teacher of the 13th Dalai Lama. His publication "The Tibetan Book of Living and Dying" makes the Buddhist path easily accessible for people in the West.

Tantra Term for the scriptures of Vajrayana and Tantrism.

Tara The most important female meditation deity and a bodhisattva. Legend has it that she was born from one of Avalokiteshvara's tears, thus representing highest compassion as well.

Thich Nhat Hanh Contemporary meditation master from Vietnam. Important representative of Buddhism in the West.

Tilopa 988–1069. Indian tantric, Naropa's master.

Tsongkhapa 1357–1419. Losang Dragpa. Initiator of the Gelugpa order.

Vajra Tibetan: dorje. Diamond sceptre, ritual implement which symbolizes method, selfless activity for the benefit of all sentient beings.

Vajrayana Diamond vehicle. Tantrism, mainly practiced in Tibetan society.

Acknowledgements & Imprint

Bibliography

Sogyal Rinpoche, The Tibetan Book of Living and Dying. San Francisco 1992

Sogyal Rinpoche, Glimpse After Glimpse: Daily Reflections on Living and Dying. San Francisco 1995

Hildegard von Bingen, Scivias. Wisse die Wege. Freiburg 1990

Dalai Lama, Eine Politik der Güte. Düsseldorf 1992

Dalai Lama, Zeiten des Friedens. Freiburg 1994

Dalai Lama, Drukpa Rinpoche, Tibetische Weisheiten. München

Dhammapada, Die Weisheitslehren des Buddha. Freiburg

Albert Einstein, Aus meinen späten Jahren. Stuttgart 1959

Gautama Buddha, Worte lebendiger Stille. Freiburg 2000

Gautama Buddha, Die vier edlen Wahrheiten. München 1997

Anthony de Mello, Eine Minute Weisheit. Freiburg 2000

Rainer Maria Rilke, Worte, die verwandeln. Freiburg 1996

Antoine de Saint-Exupéry, Flug nach Arras. Düsseldorf 1959

Albert Schweitzer, Worte über das Leben. Freiburg 1990

Mother Teresa, Wie ein Tropfen im Ozean. München 2001

Thich Nhat Hanh, Zeiten der Achtsamkeit. Freiburg 2001

Thich Nhat Hanh, Worte der Hinwendung. Freiburg

We are very grateful to Geshe Lama Ngawang Changchup for his support and his trust in our work. Many thanks to Karma Namgyal for taking care of everything locally. Special thanks to Ms Irmtraut Wäger of "Deutsche Tibet Hilfe" in Munich, a German Tibet support group, for helping with her contacts in Dharamsala. Also thanks a lot to Annemarie Heitzmann (Calligraphy), Katharina Sommer (text advice "Buddhism in Ladakh"). We appreciate the support of Bernd Henrichs (Leica AG), Christine Alig and Gisela Völzke (Austrian Airlines), and Manfred Hell (Jack Wolfskin).

Photography: Dieter Glogowski & Albrecht Haag
Text: Dieter Glogowski
Translation and editing: Hannelore Wenderoth
Proof-reading: Brian Leonard
Design: Albrecht Haag; revised by Wiebke Hengst
Cartography: Gecko Maps, www.karto-atelier.com
Calligraphy: Annemarie Heitzmann
Product management: Dr. Birgit Kneip
Production: Bettina Schippel
Printed in Slovenia by MKT, Ljubljana

This work has been carefully researched by the author and kept up to date as well as checked by the publisher for coherence. However, the publishing house can assume no liability for the accuracy of the data contained herein. We are always thankful for suggestions and advice. Please write to: C.J. Bucher Publishing, Product Management, P.O. Box 80 02 40, 81602 Munich, Germany; e-mail: info@bucher-publishing.com

ISBN 978-3-7658-1584-3

See our full listing of books at
www.bucher-publishing.com

Leica my point of view